Body Language

Master the Psychological Techniques of Body Language: Enhance Your Relationships and Career Success with Proven Body Language Techniques

Richard Shay

Table of Contents

This document is geared towards providing exact and reliable information in regards to the topic and issue covered. The publication is sold with the idea that the publisher is not required to render accounting, officially permitted, or otherwise, qualified services. If advice is necessary, legal or professional, a practiced individual in the profession should be ordered.

From a Declaration of Principles which was accepted and approved equally by a Committee of the American Bar Association and a Committee of Publishers and Associations.

The information provided herein is stated to be truthful and consistent, in that any liability, in terms of inattention or otherwise, by any usage or abuse of any policies, processes, or directions contained within is the solitary and utter responsibility of the recipient reader. Under no circumstances will any legal responsibility or blame be held against the publisher for any reparation, damages, or monetary loss due to the information herein, either directly or indirectly.

Part I

Getting Started

Introduction

Body Language: Master the Psychological Techniques of Body Language is the ultimate source for obtaining tools based on research that will allow you to better understand the psychology of body language. You will learn how to become more aware of your body language subtleties (inside and out) as well as the body language of others in order to enhance your professional and personal life.

Written by a psychology professional, this book is based on clinical knowledge, evidence-based tools, and research. *Body Language: Master the Psychological Techniques of Body Language* is much more than a book...it is a program to help you master the psychological techniques of body language in your everyday life.

Topics include:

The Psychology of Body Language

What to do Under Pressure

Micro-expressions

Deception

How to Get Someone to Like You

Body Language of Leaders

First Impressions

How to Get Build Rapport Quickly

How to Get the Job, Client, Promotion, or Sale

How We are Influenced by Our Own Non-Verbals

How to Change Your Identity for the Better Using Body Language

And more...

The Psychology of Body Language

What is my body language communicating to you? What is your body language communicating to me? These are the questions many ask when it comes to how people are perceived.

There is a great deal of research to show that analyzing body language is a valid way to look at judgments. We make inferences from body language. These judgments can affect who we hire, who we promote, and who we date. A gesture that can hide a lie, a greeting can get the job, and a gesture can get the deal. Body language can impact every area of your life. In this book, we will dissect the body, the face, and the voice to reveal its hidden meanings and secrets.

In this world, what we say is important, but sometimes we are not getting all of the message. Just seven percent of communication is verbal. Ninety-three percent of what we pick up from others is non-verbal. When we think of non-verbal communication we think of how we are judged and how we judge others. On the flip side, we are also influenced by our own non-verbal communication.

Micro-expressions, postures, and handshakes all affect the way we perceive others and the way others perceive us. Despite people's best efforts, the truth can often be leaked out. Body language comes from the brain stem. The limbic system in the brain is also involved with producing body language. Somewhere down the line of history, as with most animals, we developed the ability to communicate in a non-verbal fashion. It remains our primary way to communicate especially when it comes to emotionality. Charles Darwin first wrote about the universality of emotions mainly because these and other survival aspects of ourselves are controlled by the limbic system of the brain.

The responsibilities of the limbic system include procreation, homeostasis, noticing and reacting to threats, emotions and assuring our survival. The reactions of the limbic system are immediate and consistent and apply to all of us across cultures. The reactions of the limbic system are hard-wired in us. In each culture, when we get close to the edge of the cliff we avoid coming too close to get a look over the edge. It's the limbic system in our brains that will prevent us from getting too close to danger.

Our thoughts, feelings, and needs are processed by the limbic system and they are ultimately expressed in body language. From birth, we display signs of discontent, content, and other emotions and we display these through our facial expressions and gestures similarly throughout our lives. For example, when we see someone we love, we will mirror their behavior, our pupils will dilate, and we tilt our heads. Again, our limbic

system is communicating through the body the actual feelings we hold with corresponding non-verbal communication.

Adjusting body language does not feel natural at first. Mastering body language takes practice and it takes going out of your comfort zone at times. One of the ways we learn is by mimicking what is modeled for us. In the case of body language, we want to mimic the body language of successful speakers, successful business moguls, successful daters etc. Ultimately, when it comes to the psychology of body language, not only can you shift how others view you (by faking body language until it becomes natural) you can also shift the way you feel yourself because of your new body language in the long-term.

During this journey, you will become equipped with the tools to analyze body language. By the end of this book, every moment you spend with others (personal or professional), will become impactful and powerful. The secret world of body language is about to be opened for you.

First Impressions

Should you trust your first impression?

Research in social psychology asserts that we are quick to form lasting impressions of others based on their behaviors which largely includes body language. A clumsy step can help us predict how a person is going to behave in the future. A gesture, facial expression, or someone's posture can make us believe that we can expect more of the same from that person in the future. That said, we can also change our impressions in light of new information. Fortunately, "Impression Updating" can help alter a negative first impression at a later time. However, impression updating can take time and it is simply easier to be cognizant of body language for a successful first impression the first time around.

No matter how much preparation you've had before a first encounter with someone there is oftentimes anxiety that sets in at some point. It feels like no matter how much "on your game" you are, certain people you meet can leave feeling sort of indifferent about you. Why does that happen and how much time do you have to make a good impression? The answer is you have very little time which makes it all that more important to be aware of the impressions you make with your body language.

Whether you realize it or not, your brain is filing away information for continuous recall. It's called pattern recognition and it's a survival skill. You go into pattern recognition mode when you meet someone for the very first time. You take in physical features and body language and any other indicators that can help you judge that person. Your brain runs the person against all of the other people you have ever met and within a few seconds your brain rates that person of what kind of a person they are. Interestingly, your snap judgment is usually accurate according to research. However, snap judgments don't always work and are not always helpful. At the same time, these snap judgments are made which makes it critical for us to be aware of the impression we are giving with our body language.

You can decide whether you like someone or not within a fraction of a second of seeing them. You make an unconscious decision. There's a part of your brain that is called the brain stem. It makes snap judgments about everyone around you. Based on behavior, it decides whether you should retreat or approach a person. There are categories that your brain has for everyone else around you.

Your brain stem can perceive a person as a potential friend or potential enemy simply or a potential sexual partner from snap judgments. Does he look like me? Is she similar to me? Does her hair look good? We pay attention to people who are potential friends or mates.

We may also pay attention to someone we perceive as an enemy although we are then guarded. We also tend to tune out those who we subconsciously perceive as none of those things. As a result, we feel indifferent toward them. Many times, during a first meeting we feel indifferent to a stranger but it is our job to make ourselves memorable in a positive way.

Building Rapport

One of the most obvious ways to build rapport with someone is to smile. However, there is a proper way to smile to instill trust and get the other person to match you. You want to narrow the eyes and smile. Smiling with the eyes is important to convey genuineness. The ideal smile will build for three seconds and be sustained for three seconds. Then you want to flash up the eyebrows eye brows. This elicits the feeling from the other person that you are a friend or a friend of the family. It triggers the primitive brain and it produces the feeling that you know them from somewhere and that you are liked.

IMPORTANCE OF PROPER HAND SHAKES

Handshakes are not universal. Not everyone shakes hands to greet. However, in some places handshakes are critically important. When you meet people for the very first time you decide in the first four minutes or less whether you are going to hear them out or whether you are going to reject them and their message. There are different feelings that are elicited when a person shakes hands with another person. One is "I feel like I could get along with this one". Another is a gut feeling that "This person cannot be trusted."

During a handshake, the angle of the hand is important. If someone shakes your hand and their hand ends up on top you will likely get a gut feeling that the person is trying to dominate and you would be correct. Ideally, unless you are trying to win a political race, you want to neither have the hand on top nor bottom. You want to shake hands up and down with each being at equal sides.

Whether you are preparing for a date or a meeting or a presentation, consider how much impact you are having with your hands. A handshake is about how aggressive or passive a person is or the person's potential for harm. It also conveys how alive or energized a person feels. A person that shakes your hand will check whether or not the handshake is passive, aggressive, friendly, or unfriendly. A limp handshake indicates to someone that a person is not engaged or bored or uninterested. You want to give out as much pressure as another person is giving you. This is a mirroring or matching technique. This helps with building rapport. If you are unable to feel the palm of someone's hands the handshake will not feel comfortable. You will, in fact, likely see a rolling of the eyes (a disgust gesture) if you do not feel the palm of someone's hand. So, make sure to press the palm of your hand to their hand.

Likeability and attractiveness can be established in a fraction of a second. Full open body language says that you have nothing to hide. Every good speaker (whether in a meeting or on a date) expresses from the heart by gesturing to the heart once in a while. Also, it is important to gesture just a second before you make a statement. When we are speaking truthfully, we gesture about a half second before we speak so if you want to come off truthful do the same.

What you do not want to do is rub your hands or any part of the body for that matter. Self-touch gesture means that a person is feeling in some way uncomfortable. Remember to connect with eye contact. Make sure to convey natural confidence not over-confidence.

Show your hands. This indicates to a person "I come unarmed". Open body language indicates that you are not a predator so expose your belly when you are interacting with another person. You want to be perceived as being honest and good to be around. Hands all the way down by the side looks sleepy or disengaged. It's a mistake to allow your hands hang by your side. Hands should be up (with palms up) to display truthfulness and engagement. Ideally, you want to be gesturing at stomach height without blocking the stomach. Concentrate on your performance of the content more than just the content. The question you want to ask yourself is what you can do to enhance the content you already have in order to build rapport and get your message across.

Exercise for You:

Do an audit of your body right now. Are you hunching? Crossing your ankles? Are you spread out? Are you holding your arm? What are you doing with your body right now? Write down what you notice now.

_____
_____
_____
_____
_____
_____
_____
_____
_____
_____
_____
_____
_____
_____
_____

Part II

Power Positioning

Body Language of Leaders

Leaders make strong body language statements (i.e. the faster you stride the more powerful you are perceived). However, it is not simply speed of walking that demonstrates how powerful one is perceived. Animal power walking with shoulders bouncing back and forth can be a sign of power. Traditional American power movements involve very little movement above the shoulders which appears controlled. Perceiving the body language of powerful leaders can be straightforward but body language is often complex and misunderstood.

Successful leaders often have an enhanced ability to spot body language well. There is a correlation between a salesperson's ability to read body language their ability to sell. Another skill that leaders have is the ability to be conscious with their body language. They seem to know which body language behaviors to do and which ones to avoid at any given time. Grabbing someone on the elbow also demonstrates dominance. Little tap at the end for good measure demonstrates they hold power and the other is a "good little boy" or "good little girl". The center figure in a picture always appears to us as the more important figure. Politicians know this fact very well and position themselves to take advantage of this fact.

One thing a person would want to avoid is displaying negative emotions on a face (for example wrinkling of the nose and raising of the one side of the lip which is a display of disgust). When someone is trying to convey a positive message, facial expressions displaying disgust would obviously be an incongruency and if done together would appear deceptive. One lip going up is a look of contempt or superiority. This would be a micro-expression you would see on a person at the beginning of a negotiation. Another skill that leaders have is that they are able to elicit body language behaviors in others by adjusting how they interact with them to get a desired response.

If you are watching someone speak and their back is turned, or if they are self-soothing by wringing their hands, or they are looking up and down and fidgeting, you will notice that they are uncomfortable. The last thing we want at a negotiation or a pitch is to be perceived as nervous or uncomfortable in anyway. As we know, communication begins before you even open your mouth. Someone's first impression of you is your position and your posture. Perhaps it is obvious, but you should stand facing your audience. It is also critical to be aware of where you are standing. Around the center of the room or stage is ideal. You want to avoid being in the corner. Facing away from the window is also key so that your eye contact does not shift outside making you appear disengaged and disinterested. Avoid putting your hands in your pockets. It is difficult to convey a strong message from this position. Always keep your hands in sight.

The power person says "I'm in control" by making the other person walk through the door first. The last man or woman through the door is the winner. Even when friends meet, subtle body language can reveal who has the power. If one is hosting, they can become very territorial. They go through the door last and helps guest through the door with a hand on the back to display dominance. Place your feet hip width apart. Gesture from the sides of your belly with palms up to elicit trust from the audience or any person in front of you. Some people believe you should gesture from your hands all the way down at your sides. However, if you want to build rapport it is wise to gesture from belly up, however, be careful to not block your belly when you are gesturing. If you block your stomach you will be perceived either as uncomfortable or as someone that should not be trusted.

According to research studies, when a speaker is asking the audience to do something 84 percent of the audience will comply if the gesture is palm up. On the contrary, if a speaker gestures by pointing the finger at them, only twenty-eight percent of the audience will comply. So, never point your fingers at the audience or the person with whom you are meeting. Lastly, make sure that your gestures look natural and loose. As a speaker, or as a presenter at a meeting, we can be hyper-focused on our own body language that we forget about the body language of the one hearing the message. As a speaker and as a leader, it is your responsibility to be aware of the body language signals of the other person.

Negotiation

When we are negotiating with someone for something we need to be aware of body language. With negotiation comes excitement, disgust, contempt, and sometimes deceit. You want to know what a person's body language is at baseline. Therefore, it is useful to view a video of that person before you go into a negotiation with them.

During negotiation, avoid blinking too much. Maintain eye contact when you introduce yourself. Match their grip of the handshake and make three pumps of the handshakes. You want to use proxemics. The safe space is four feet away. Any closer can be invasive and any further away can feel too distant. You also want to avoid sitting straight across from the other person as well. Ideally, you want a bit of an angle but still facing the other with your entire body.

Because a negotiation is typically carried out face-to-face, there are many messages sent and received that are not spoken. These messages are sent through your behavior, whether you arrive late or early, the clothes you wear, facial expressions, your posture, and your gestures. The effective use of body language can really help to make your message optimal.

Begin a negotiation by appearing friendly. A friendly face hides your true plans for a negotiation. Make them comfortable by being friendly but not overly friendly. After you greet them and sit down you want to appear neutral and relaxed during the actual negotiation. You do not want to leak secrets from your face. A person with a poker face is hard to read. However, lack of eye contact can make people feel you are being dishonest or disengaged. If there are other members of the team you are negotiating with you want to ensure that you make eye contact with them in addition to the head negotiator. This way you are not alienating other decision makers.

Make your initial offer with a calm demeanor, neutral face or friendly face leaning forward. Speak clearly and be careful not to talk too fast as you will appear anxious. Show surprise when you hear the counter offer. This indicates this is not in your comfort zone. If you lean backwards you are displaying disinterest. If you lean forward you are displaying interest so lean forward when you want to reinforce the other person.

If you want to make a point that this is your "rock bottom" offer and you want the other side to believe you it will be important to signal as such. For instance, you want to gesture a half a second before you make the statement not after. It is critical to gesture a half second before you speak so that it appears natural. If it is authentic to what you are saying you will notice that your gesture begins just before you speak. Authentic limbic responses of discomfort or comfort will be reflected in the body so be aware of what you are saying with it and what others are as well.

Reinforcement during Negotiation

Use your facial expressions and gestures to send the message you want to convey during a negotiation. If you hear the other side agreeing with you or mentioning a price you like you want to reinforce the other person. Positively reinforce them by smiling genuinely and/or nodding your head. Remember to only match and mirror them when they are using open body language. In order to get what you want during a proposal it is critical to be mindful of hand gestures. Studies have shown that if you ask something of someone with your palms up you have a significantly better chance of getting the other person to comply. This means that instead of pointing your finger at them or gesturing with palms down, it is critical to make the request with palms up. This will help get you what it is that *you want*.

Dealing Under Pressure

During high pressure moments you will notice "tells". Standing with hands behind the back or holding your wrists and stroking own fingers tells yourself "I can get through this." While this is a way to self-soothe, it also conveys either dishonesty or discomfort or both. It indicates that a person is feeling under pressure with moderate to high levels of anxiety. They may be trying to protect themselves from being found out and getting through difficult questions.

When someone makes a definitive statement and immediately retreats we know they are not telling the truth. For example, a person makes a statement then backs up and crosses arms. This indicates defensive body language. You can be confident that they are not being honest at that point in the conversation.

Everyone's body language is different. Everyone has their own quirks so body language analysts will look for what is normal for a particular person in a particular situation. They will analyze what the person does when you are asking them neutral questions about their lives. Then, you will have a norm to compare with other questions. If an investigator is investigating a crime, they will ask what is a normal response for someone being asked that same question (like whether or not they killed a spouse).

When we are in trouble, we cover our eyes. Celebrities who are not a fan of attention will put on glasses whether day or night. Under this type of intense scrutiny, a public figure's body language often needs to be advised by professionals. Politicians, similar to celebrities, are always in the spotlight. There are some that are genius when they mess up. They regress and become child-like. It's likeable and playful. In 1960 Nixon and Kennedy were running for president. "The Great Debate" was the first televised debate and it was between the two. It was the moment when candidates realized they needed to focus on their visual image. Nixon appeared less controlled compared to Kennedy in the televised debate. Kennedy allowed makeup to be applied. Nixon refused makeup and began sweating. Nixon won the debate with the radio audience. However, the audience that viewed the televised debate favored Kennedy. He appeared more controlled and confident. Voters observed their every move while they were under pressure.

Body language is a critical component for someone who is trying to shape an image. Oftentimes, a body language consultant will ask the client "Who is someone you admire?" A person will many times hunch over when they feel threatened. When not threatened they stand up straight. You can tell when someone is coached when their gestures do not seem natural. They appear as if they think before they gesture. When speaking, it is important to gesture a half second before you speak. Gesture to your

heart to appear grateful for applause to convey
genuineness.

Exercise for You:

For the next two minutes, practice a couple of the body language techniques you have learned so far and write down how it makes you feel (calm, confident, powerful etc.).

_____

_____

_____

_____

_____

_____

_____

_____

_____

_____

_____

_____

_____

How to Deal with Difficult Situation Successfully

To show that you are in integrity, your face, your head, your body, and your gestures must be in alignment. If you gesture in one direction and look in another direction there is an incongruency and a disconnect. This can lead people to see you as being deceptive.

For police, reading body language can mean life or death. Police officers are continuously evaluating individuals based on body language. The first thing police look at are the eyes. They also want to see if a person is fidgety, hands are moving, or they are looking in the rear view mirror a lot. These are "tells" that a person may be guilty. Hands in pockets tells you that a person is nervous about what is going to happen or he is about to become aggressive or pull something out of his pocket. Clapping the hands is one of the last indicators you see before someone is about to fight. It's critical for police officers to read body language so that they can recognize a threat and prevent getting hurt. There are situations when body language needs to be evaluated in a fraction of a second.

Researchers have dissected the thousands of expressions that appear on the face. They have decoded the expressions that we use. Dr. Paul Ekman conducted a study that compared the facial expressions that crossed cultures. The study compared emotions of facial expressions with those in Japan and New Guinea and western countries. He made videos of these people making expressions of sadness, surprise, contempt, happiness, anger, fear and disgust. Ekman's facial research had a significant impact on the study of body language. We now have a face reader which uses the seven basic emotions established by Ekman that maps the muscles of the face to read facial expressions. Every expression is given a different degree of the expression of emotion (disgust etc.). It is used in advertising and in security. The face communicates even more than the seven basic emotions. We react both consciously and unconsciously to the expressions we see on others.

Our eyes tell more than we think. When we are excited, our eyes dilate. Pokers players don't want you to see their excitement and they hide their eyes by looking down or wearing sunglasses. We know about the seven universal emotions. Emotion shows on the face but we know how to fake it. If the emotion on the face lasts more than one second you are most likely faking it. Another clear marker of deception is flipping of the tongue.

When we lie we tend to do movements with our hands that we might not typically. The first is that we cover our mouths. Second, we scratch our nose. We scratch our nose when we lie because our adrenaline increases making us itchy. We also tend to rub our neck or our ears when we are being deceptive or when we are stressed. Stress is often an indicator of deception. We always gesture first then speak. When we lie, we say the words first and then we gesture. One of the classic clips was when former President Bill Clinton made the famous statement "I did not have sexual relations with that woman." He gestures after he makes the statement indicating that he is being deceptive according to experts in body language. We want to examine where the hands go, where the palms are facing, and the timing of the movement. When we lie, we tend to do movements with our hands we wouldn't otherwise. When someone is lying they tend to hide their palms by putting them in their pockets, putting them behind their backs, or gesturing with palms down. We say a great deal without saying anything.

When we attempt to control our bodies to deceive, many of us focus on facial expressions and the upper body and we often forget about what we are doing with our feet and what others are doing with their feet. Crossing of the legs, feet, or ankles is an indicator that one is uncomfortable about what one is saying. It may be indication that a person is holding back valuable information. If a person is shifting from leg to leg or rocking oneself they are most likely nervous or uncomfortable. A lot of feet movement is another indicator of discomfort. This is a sign that a person is attempting to self-soothe.

Men tend to lie more to appear more powerful and to appear more successful and interesting. Women tend to lie to protect others but of course this is not the only reason. If you would like to know if someone wants to exit a conversation look at their feet. The direction of feet is a sign of how much a person wants to talk with another person. If a person's torso is pointed toward you and their foot or feet are pointing toward the exit, it likely means that the person is wanting to exit the conversation. Conversely, if weight is equally distributed on both legs it indicates that you are comfortable about what you are saying and you are taking a firm stance with regard to your statements. Never forget the importance of feet when you want to convey honesty and when you are looking for deceit in another. It is important to convey openness with body language, with a firm stance, and little movement when it comes to the feet. Finally, when someone makes a positive statement but shakes their head no that is a "tell" that someone is lying.

MICRO-EXPRESSIONS

We are hard-wired to understand three thousand plus facial expressions. Micro-expressions are those expressions that come out for a fraction of a second. They are rare and they can show that a person is trying to conceal something. Micro-expressions can be a twenty fifth of a second. Micro-expressions give away how you feel in a particular situation. Brows would come down if you are angry because you are being accused of something you didn't do. On the other hand, if one is being accused of doing something they actually did their brows might come up and together. This would indicate that fear and surprise leaking. When you see the jaws clenched or the nostrils flare this can be a sign of aggression.

When people are being authentic, you are taken to their level. You see their expressions as less forced and more genuine whether angry, saddened, or ecstatic. Thinking leads to emotions and emotions lead to behavior (or in this case micro-expression). Emotions manifest themselves in the face as micro-expressions.

The VOICE

Tone and pitch, speed, and rhythm are all important indicators. Thirty-eight percent of our communication is tone of voice. People judge others simply by how low or high a voice tone sounds. Research shows that a woman's voice affects the emotional parts of a man's brain. The higher the pitch the less credibility a voice is given according to studies. This is why consultants will often advise politicians to bring their voices lower pitch. Voices become lower as we become older. A good speaker will get you to join in with the rhythm and cadence of their voice. They may also speak on a beat. A speaker similar to a Baptist preacher would starts down low, build up, use a long pause and build more. It's powerful because the content is no longer as important and the speaker tells you what you should feel...something very powerful.

As we speak and think about what we are saying, our brains sends messages to our voice box. They have been categorized into inaccuracies or probable falses in technology called voice analysis. The higher the number in certain values the more of a chance of dishonesty. How you sit, how you dress, how you walk tells you whether you are a sheep or a wolf. It's ironic how little we invest into the actual content. When there is a contrast between the words and the body language, always believe the body language.

Part III

Body Language for Likeability and Attraction

How to Tell if Someone Likes You

Preening is an indicator that someone likes you or wants to impress you. Preening is any adjustment in your appearance. Some people think preening is just for women but it's not. Men and women preen which is a pacifying action. Men and women typically preen when they are attracted to someone and when the want to make a good impression.

A hair preen can be very quick (a quick stroke of the hair or a quick hair flip). The moving of hair by men or women is an example of preening. Another form of preening is straightening one's clothes. If you see a man or woman straightening the shirt of pants, this is an example of adjusting the appearance. Smoothing one's clothes is another sign of bringing attention to oneself. It can be a sign of wanting to present well and it can even be a sign of attraction. Jewelry adjustment also happens a great deal when one is attracted to another. A man may adjust his watch or his cufflinks. A woman may adjust her watch, necklace, or earrings.

Indicators of Interest (IOIs) are body language "tells" that convey that a person is interested in another person. Producing an approach tell (like one of the preening gestures previously discussed) is a way to invite another person to introduce him/herself. A man will puff out his chest or find ways to take up more space with his arms or legs. Men and women will also make a lot of eye contact. Studies show that we look at people we are attracted for longer periods of time than those we are not. People who are attracted to you will look for ways to touch you. They will also tend to become close in proximity. He/she may touch you on the small of the back or the shoulder. A man will stand tall expanding the shoulders and a woman may also shift her hips when she walks from side to side which shows off the curves of her body.

It is important for men to refrain from approaching women from the back as this puts them on the defense. You want to approach women from the side or the front. Men are more likely to approach a woman who appears available. This means a smile, open body language, showing off the neck, looking up to the side at the man. Research shows that men don't pick up on body language as well as women. On average, men miss body language signals three times during a situation. This makes it important for women wanting to attract men to engage in at least three indicators of interest for the man to ensure you are interested.

People who like you will tilt their head and smile. Women who are attracted to you will also draw attention to their neck. The reason is that they are exposing pheromones. This is also attractive to a man because it shows the roundness of a woman's face. Women will flick their hair or touch their hair which is another indicator that they are attracted to someone. When women feel aroused they will massage the top of their chest just under the neck with their fingers. When any person is engaged with you they will point their torso toward you. Women may raise their eyes and lower their lids. Whether you are a man or a woman, if you want to convey power you want to take up as much space as possible by taking elbow space and spreading legs when standing, crossing legs with one foot on the knee etc. Eyes will dilate in both men and women when they find a person attractive. If you are attempting to build rapport with someone it is important to keep body language open (so arms uncrossed) and have an expressive face. Leave your hands loosened up and gesture with palms up and smile. People view others with open with their body language as more attractive overall.

How to Get Someone to Like You

Researchers found that people can make instance comparisons between two people next to each other and decide who is more competent. In one study, people took only seconds to choose photographs of political candidates to judge their competence. More than seventy percent of the faces they chose turned out to be the ones elected. Expressions that communicate competence are a genuine smile "a nice smile". No smile has been shown to indicate less competence. Eye contact is also a sign of competence.

People like others that are similar to them. When two people like each other they subconsciously begin to "match" or "mirror" the other's body language. You can turn this around and actually begin to match or mirror someone's body language in order to get them to like you in the first place. This technique works for anyone who is trying to get a colleague, interviewer, acquaintance, or romantic interest to like you.

Science asserts that mirror neurons exist. As humans, we mirror each other. We copy each other. One of the best way to get engaged in a group is to copy others in their mannerisms, voice volume, gestures etc. However, if someone has closed body language it is not advised to mirror their body language. You are not going to choose body language that contradicts your goal of opening someone up. If the goal is to open the person up, to sell them on an idea, to win them over etc. you will need to remain open in order to be perceived as truthful and engaged. You, at that point, will be modeling for them what you want them to feel

until their body language matches yours. You will smile, have open gestures, nod your head. Every time the other does an open behavior your will smile even more and match that positive body language behavior. This, in turn, will reinforce their open body language resulting in them to feel more open and display more openness.

You can match someone's breathing, timing of gestures, almost anything they do. Remember to not make it to obvious. If you see someone picking up their drink pick up yours. If they turn slightly turn similarly. Getting into sync with people makes it that much easier to break down barriers and become liked by whomever you are around and it is based on research.

How We are Influenced by Our Own Non-Verbals

Non-verbal expressions of dominance can be very impactful in both personal and professional life. When we stretch out, take up space we are displaying dominance. When we put our hands behind our head and lean back we are showing dominance. We do this naturally when we have power and also when we are feeling powerful in the moment. When we feel powerless, we close up we make ourselves small. When someone is displaying power in their non-verbals we tend not to mirror we tend to make ourselves smaller. We see another powerful display of non-verbal communication and we collapse our bodies in response. This seems to be related to gender. Women are more likely to make their bodies take up less space than men. However, powerful poses can be highly beneficial for those who do them.

Can faking it lead to feeling more powerful? The answer is yes.

Our non-verbal communication does influence how we feel about ourselves and a situation. When you feel powerful you are more likely to expand your body language. It is also true that if you expand your body language (spread out, take up space) you feel more powerful. Powerful individuals tend to feel confident and more optimistic. They take more risks. Physiologically speaking, high power alpha males have high testosterone and low cortisol levels. Power is not only about testosterone but also more resistant to stress thus having low cortisol levels in response to stress. Role changes can shift a mindset and thus the body language.

Folding up your arms or hunching over and making yourself small is a low power pose. Spreading your elbows out, puffing the chest out, etc. are high power poses. Hormonal changes configure your brain to either be stress reactive and feeling shut down to being comfortable and powerful. Power posing can change your life in significant ways. Power poses can be useful when giving a pitch, giving a speech, or going through a job interview.

Typically, before a job interview people will hunch over, look at their phone, cross their arms etc. Essentially their body language becomes small. According to research studies, the people who pose in high power poses before the interview were chosen for the job. The factors that affect whether someone will be hired include being perceived (remember the operative word being perceived) as passionate, confident, enthusiastic, authentic, comfortable, and captivating. We can show these traits through body language.

We can literally shift our moods, confidence-level and ultimately our identities by changing our non-verbal communication.

Take two minutes before going into any social situation, professional meeting. Power pose before the meeting. If you feel uncomfortable, open your body language anyway and keep it open so that you can build rapport and so that you don't miss out on an opportunity.

Whether in business, at home, or in relationships, always ask yourself am I displaying discomfort or comfort? Ask yourself, is the person I am speaking to displaying comfort or discomfort?

By focusing on this it will lead you to explore issues that are concealed, or to verify the validity of statements expressed. We are constantly transmitting information as to our thoughts, intentions, and feelings through our limbic responses. Most likely the behaviors you see will fit under one of these two categories (comfort or discomfort) for which we can thank that emotional part of the brain: the limbic system.

Conclusion

Your thoughts leak out into your body language. People are unconsciously and consciously able to recognize how you feel about them, how much you are withholding, and whether or not you like them. You can change your thoughts so that your body language naturally reflects your mindset or you can be aware of all of the body language "tells" so that you display what it is you want shown. Body language cannot only change others' opinions about you but it can also help you positively affect how you feel about yourself leaving you more successful your romantic and professional life.

You are now equipped with evidence-based tools to help you understand the psychology of body language, how to use it to your advantage, and how to maintain proper body language for an edge in life.

Thank you for reading!

-Richard Shay